Contents

In the Name of Allah,
The Most Merciful,
The Eternally
Compassionate.

Why?

Peace be upon you, my dearly beloved friend. That's an excellent question! Never stop asking that. Alhamdulillah (All praise and thanks to God) that we are able to reconnect like this.

Nothing is random.

There is a reason you picked up this book, just like there is a reason I picked up the pen to write it. First and foremost, all good is truly from Allah, and the mistakes are only my own human fallibility (Quran 4:79). If you find a mistake, please do write me. I will be forever indebted in gratitude.

I hope that this humble servant of yours has been able to convey something of benefit. If so, I request you to pray for me. Please pray that Allah Allows this book to be an ongoing charity for me. Pray that it is a witness for me on the Day of Judgment that I was not afraid of anyone but Him.

This book is my hope to share the favors you have so generously gifted me. By His Mercy. May Allah Grant you all the absolute best of this life and the real life, after this one (Al-Akhira).

You will forever be in my prayers.

As I sit here, in my room, with the window open to feel the early morning breeze, my eyes well up with tears.

This seems like a dream.

Up until last week, if you said to me that I would be writing, let alone publishing a book, I would not believe you. You see, most of my life, I had imprisoned myself by my mistakes, both big and small. I did not dare to fly because I thought I would hopelessly fall to the ground.

I begged and I pleaded. I became nothing.

Allah Showed me how His Endless Love and Mercy was infinitely greater than my greatest weakness.

He Gave me wings to see why the caterpillar had been a butterfly the moment He Said "Be."

In every breath, He Showed me how He Had Been there all along.

You know, I did not plan this to have any poetry. I had all my notes for a novel, you see.

But we plan, and Allah Plans. And Allah Is The Best of Planners! (Quran 8:30)

And so, after six years of continuous jihad, of struggles and failures, in the seventh year, here I am. Free, free, free, at last!

I cannot hold it inside anymore, lest I forget how to breathe. Allah Has Brought me back to life.

It's not who I am, dear friend, it is just who He Is.

My Beloved Allah Tells us: "Oh mankind, you are those in need of Allah, while Allah Is The Free of Need, The Praiseworthy!" (Quran 35:15)

And yet, He Gives and Gives and Gives. It is only we who get tired of asking. SubhanAllah! Glorified is my Allah Above all they associate with Him!

My dearly beloved friend, no matter who you are or where you're from, let's continue this journey. From Love, with Love and back to Love.

I want to show you what is possible when we open the windows, as my beloved Allah Has Shown me.

Here, take my hand. We will do this.
We will see the sun rise, together.

I am, because we are.

Allahumma yassir walaa tu'assir. Rabbi tammim bi khair.

Ya Allah, make it easy and do not make it difficult.
My Master, My Caretaker, my endless Gift-Giver,
make it end well.
Ameen.

I did not write this book. It wrote me.

A Prayer

In the Name of Allah, The Most Merciful,
The Eternally Compassionate.
Wa akhiru da'wana an al-hamdu li-Llahi rabb il-'alamin!
Was-salatu was-salamu 'ala rasulihil-karim!
Rabbana taqabbal minna innaka antas-Sami' ul-'Alim!
Subhana Rabbuka rabb ul-'izzati 'amma yasifun.
Wa salamun 'alal-mursalin.
Wal-hamdu li-Llahi rabb il-'alamin!
Ameen!

In the end our claim is that all praise and thanks
is for Allah, the Lord of all the Worlds,
and blessings and greetings to the Prophet (saw),
Our Lord! Accept from us this duty!
Indeed, You, only You, are The Hearer, The Knower!
Gloried is my Lord, the Lord of Majesty, Above all
they attribute (to Him)!
Peace be upon His messengers!
Praise and thanks be to Allah
The Lord of all the Worlds! Ameen!

Let Thy Will Be Done.

On Light and Breath

"And remember when your Lord said to the angels,
I am going to create a human being from sounding clay
molded from black mud, So, when I have proportioned him
and breathed into him the soul which I created for him,
then fall yourselves down prostrating
yourselves to him ..."
(Qur'an 15:28-29)

∞∞∞

Let's start from the beginning, shall we? The earthly beginning, that is. Let's find some common ground, you and me. Us.

∞∞∞

But before we begin, let's take a deep breath. Inhale. All the way back to your throat. Can you feel it in your chest? Breathe in...Al...breathe out...lah. Allah. Allah. Allah. In every breath. The secret of all existence, hidden in plain sight.

Breathing is something you and I are doing right now, whether we're aware of it or not. But the remarkable thing is, we could not always breathe on our own.

Before we joined the ranks of the mortals, we had a very

cozy incubation period in the *rahm*, or womb of our mother. It was that womb that supplied food, water, and oxygen to us when we were just a seed.

Before we could do anything to deserve such pure love, we survived and thrived between its loving arms.

It gave us exactly what it knew we would need. Our mother's love sustained us before it knew what color or shape we would be, or if and how we would smile with our teeth. By His Mercy, Love fed us directly so we could get ready for the next stage of life - the stage in which we would have to breathe on our own.

> *"Allah—surely nothing is hidden from Him in the earth or in the heaven. He it is who shapes you in the wombs as He likes; there is no god but He, the Mighty, the Wise."* (Quran 3:5-6)

∞∞∞

Do you remember? No, neither do I, but science has shown us that this is what happens. So we must believe. You and I, we are science-minded people. We trust science will reveal what we need to see...eventually.

Let's continue our journey. After some arbitrary period of time, we descended from the womb through the birth canal. Deep breaths, they told our mother. Screaming from the burning pain of separation to anyone who could hear us, we entered this world. By His Mercy. A new reality...for now.

> *"And Allah has extracted you from the wombs of your mothers not knowing a thing, and He made for you hearing and vision and intellect that perhaps you would be grateful."* (Quran 16:78)

∞∞∞

Then...well, we didn't need help to breathe anymore. But even after they cut the umbilical cord, the love continued to pour. Day after day, we cried and cried in absolute fright! We screamed to be cleaned and fed throughout the night.

The love that had lovingly fed us in the womb stayed up day after day, night after night. She sacrificed her own food and rest, so that we would be taken care of just right. By His Mercy... just you wait and see.

This pure love sustained us, and cherished us, cuddled us and played with us, before we could speak even a single word of thanks. Before we even knew we were being taken care of. It took care of us so that we could be ready for the next stage of life – the stage in which we would have to feed ourselves. By His Mercy, just you wait and see...

> *"And We settle in the wombs whom We will*
> *for a specified term, then We bring you out*
> *as a child, and then [We develop you] that you may*
> *reach your [time of] maturity."* (Quran 22:5)

∞∞∞

Love continued to nurture us. It not only fed us, it taught us how to feed. It not only spoke to us, it taught us how to speak. It not only read to us, it taught us how to read. It gently held our hands as we learned to walk. It never let go...even when we fell down, this way, and that way. Again and again. And yet, again.

Slowly but surely, just as we began to breathe and learned to feed, we began to stand on our own two feet. We were Love's dearly beloved seed. And yet, despite us being able to self-support, this pure love continued to pour.

Day after day, night after night, we cried out. It was hard to do this alone, we felt whispers of doubt. Yes, we could speak, but all we did was scream. Yes, we could feed, but we did not want to fulfill our body's needs!
We refused to breathe, forgot how to sleep, drink and eat!

In our heart of hearts, we knew.
Love would always come to the rescue!

So, the love that had been taking care of us all along clothed us in mercy. It continued to cook and to clean, both for you and for me. On nights that we would forget to eat, Love fed us ever so gently. It would remind us to take good care of our sleep, to drink well, and to eat.

Breathlessly...we forgot Love's name. Even when it
pushed our hands away from the burning flames.

Where are you going, dear seed? Did you forget
how much you are in need? I Only Seek to Relieve your
burden, you see. Turn to Me, turn to Me.

Love always stood tall, eye-to-eye against anyone
who made us feel small.

My love, let it be known. You will never, ever be alone.

With Love's help, taller we grew, and it continued
to love us because love was all it knew.

And then one day, we woke up with a scream and a shout!
It seemed the burning flame of love had been put out!
It was the loneliest day in world history.
Oh! there would be no end to the misery!
We pierced our hearts with the disloyal knife!

There weren't enough trees in the world to bring love back to life!

We would never be loved, never have a true friend.
We would never, ever love again.

We were feverish with the deepest unrest.
In the darkness of the darkest night,
the sweat of shame dampened our chest.
For we had not seen love for what it was.
We had just blindly seen what it so lovingly does.

That is, till we grew apart.
Such a burning pain in our chest,
our heart!

The clocks could never turn back time!
The sun would never again shine!
Misery had been written in our fate.
Such blasphemy we would state!

So, we closed our windows,
drew the curtains real tight.
Tossing and turning
into the darkness
of the darkest night.

On Light and The Heart

"…the Day when neither wealth nor children will be of any benefit, when the only one who will be saved is the one who comes before Allah with a heart devoted to Him." (Quran 26:88-89)

∞∞∞

And then one day, we woke up.
We felt, by the window, a
cloth peeking from a
broken
empty
cup…

We snatched it from where it lay and held it close.
It was a silky soft, a beautiful red rose.
Between our tired fingers, it felt just like home.
Of a time before we thought we were forever alone.

We rubbed our tear-streaked eyes
with a heartbreaking sigh.
It was still dark outside.

Like never before, our chests began to heave.
As the oxygen rushed in, we began to breathe.
Once more, we found out, we could see, see, see!

Over the fairly large window,
cobwebs had appeared.
Breathing shakily through our nose,
humility rightfully seared.

We held the cloth to our chest real tight.
We promised to never again disappear into the night.
Tears tore through our body as we cleaned and we cleaned.
It was then that we knew we would soon be free, free, free!

The sky outside was dark,
we saw the clouds welled up with rain.
Oxygen began to roar through our veins.

Shyly, we reached out.
There was not
a single scream or shout.
We felt it once more...
Love's Life-Giving Pour.

But then we got tired of the rain.
And soon enough,
the sun came out,
once again.
As we continued to breathe,
we took in scents of such
incredible beauty.
It looked like a scene from a fairytale story.
We could finally see nature in her full glory!
Flowers of all shapes and colors,
red, orange, pink, white and blue...
we could even hear the birds chirping, too!
Into the sky, they flew and they flew!

On Light and Home

"...(Lit is such a Light) in houses, which
Allah Has Permitted to be raised to honor;
for the celebration, in them, of His name:
In them, He Is Glorified in the mornings and
in the evenings, (again and again). (Quran 24:36)

∞∞∞

And then one day, we woke up.
Clutching our empty little cup.

The caress of the early morning breeze
had come through the open window,
from out beyond the seven seas.

It held out its Gentle Hand and
we got on our knees,
In our last, deepest breath,
out flew a seed!

Into the most brilliant glittering
Light, at last, we felt freed!
Home, we realized,
is what the heart needs.

∞∞∞

Open your eyes, my dear,
don't you know you are being breathed?
In an earnest prayer lies the priciest
spiritual feast!

Breathe. Breathe. Breathe.

The deeper we breathe,
the more we can drink and eat.
Breathe. Breathe.
Breathe. Take all you need.
Breathe. Breathe. Breathe.
Then share it with the world,
and so shall you be free!

"...And whatever good
you will send ahead
for your own selves,
you will find it with Allah
much better in condition,
and much greater in reward.
And seek forgiveness from Allah.
Indeed Allah is Most-Forgiving, Most-Merciful." (Quran 73:20)

Hear, hear!
There is nothing left to fear!

Open up to Love, dear seed!
Here lies the cure for the root of all anxiety.
Love's Brilliant Glittering Melody.
Love Has Promised us that,
soon we will see!

Our hearts will soon so proudly beat!
So, dear friend,
let's be free, free, free!

Love Is Truly all we need,
for Love Is the Language
of the heartbeat!
Do you see what I see?
Al...lah. Al...lah. Al...lah!

Alhamdulillah.
Alhamdulillah.
Alhamdulillah.

To my Allah Belong The Best of examples.

Ya Wadud, Ya Allah!
Ya Wadud, Ya Allah!
Ya Wadud, Ya Allah!

Surah Fatiha – The Opening

Bismillāhi r-raḥmāni r-raḥīm
(Breathe deep) 1:1 In the Name of Allah, The Most
Merciful, The Eternally Compassionate.

Al ḥamdu lillāhi rabbi l-'ālamīn
(Breathe deep) 1:2 All Praise and thanks belongs to Allah,
Master, Caretaker and Gift-Giver of All the Worlds!

Ar raḥmāni r-raḥīm
(Breathe deep) 1:3 The Most Merciful, The Eternally
Compassionate.

Māliki yawmi d-dīn
(Breathe deep) 1:4 Master of the Day of Judgement.

Iyyāka na'budu wa iyyāka nasta'īn
(Breathe deep) 1:5 You Alone we worship;
You Alone we ask for help.

Ihdinā ṣ-ṣirāṭ al-mustaqīm
(Breathe deep) 1:6 Guide us to the straight path.

Ṣirāṭ al-laḏīna an'amta 'alayhim ġayril maġḍūbi 'alayhim walāḍ
ḍāllīn
(Breathe deep) 1:7 the path of those You have blessed, those
who incur no anger and who have not gone astray.

A Prayer

In the Name of Allah, The Most Merciful,
The Eternally Compassionate.
Wa akhiru da'wana an al-hamdu li-Llahi rabb il-'alamin!
Was-salatu was-salamu 'ala rasulihil-karim!
Rabbana taqabbal minna innaka antas-Sami' ul-'Alim!
Subhana Rabbuka rabb ul-'izzati 'amma yasifun.
Wa salamun 'alal-mursalin.
Wal-hamdu li-Llahi rabb il-'alamin!
Ameen!

In the end our claim is that all praise and thanks
is for Allah, the Lord of all the Worlds,
and blessings and greetings to the Prophet (saw),
Our Lord! Accept from us this duty!
Indeed, You, only You, are The Hearer, The Knower!
Gloried is my Lord, the Lord of Majesty, Above all
they attribute (to Him)!
Peace be upon His messengers!
Praise and thanks be to Allah
The Lord of all the Worlds! Ameen!

Let Thy Will Be Done.

On Light and The Veil

"He (Satan, The Deceiver) said: I am not such that I should prostrate to a mortal whom You Have Created of the essence of black mud fashioned in shape." (15:33)

"Said He (Allah), "Then get down (out of) it (i.e. Paradise); so, in no way is it for you to be proud therein; then go out; surely you are among the belittled."" (7:13)

"He said, "My Lord, since You made me go astray, I swear that I shall beautify for them (evils) on the earth, and shall lead all of them astray, all except Your devoted servants."" (Quran 15:39-40)

∞∞∞

Whenever we hear horrific news, we ask each other, "Can you believe this is happening in the twenty-first century? Really, oh really, how can this be!" The answer is that we have failed to understand our personality. We have forgotten how to see.

For centuries, we struggled to grasp the "thing" that makes us who we are. We were so busy trying to locate "consciousness" in places near and far. In confusion, we preserved Einstein's brain. We, too, wanted such glory and fame...

∞∞∞

Labels and theories were thrown around,
all the while we had been breathing without a sound.

Just breathe. Open your eyes and see.
You may not be able to drink or to eat.

Like a humble servant, you must clean the window.
Both up high and really, really down low.
The real you is waiting to shine! Be patient.
Keep working. It'll happen in time.
Before Breath,
it was deadly still.
Potter's clay came alive,
with our One God's Will.

And when He Ordered the angels to prostrate,
Satan turned out to be the devil ingrate.

That's when racism began, you see.
When the outcast refused to get on his knees.

Do you not see the signs?
It is not the eyes, but
the hearts that are blind!

The real you is not your ego.
No, my love, no, no, no.

For heaven on earth, you won't have to look far!
Around your heart, there's a glittering star!
Like every precious thing that must be encaged,
the heart has a veil, no matter what age!
Oh, like the pericardium!
Dear seed,
how could you
forget where you're from?

Cheer up, for light is your personality!
Indeed, it is your deepest reality...
The spots on the window are just a veil, you see.
Clean, clean, dear seed. Drop to your knees.

A beggar, with sheer humility, my head
is bowed, I'm looking at my feet.
Allah, Allah, pounds my heartbeat.

Between you and your Maker,
you will soon come to know.
Soon, it is you whose cup
will overflow.
All your life, you thought you were
a tiny drop, a seed! For you,
Allah Had Saved the sea...

Glee, upon glee, upon glee!

To put it plainly, our true self is hidden beneath the veil.
Let's remember to breathe. This Light will never let us fail!

*Like makeup, our mortal
mask has been beautified.
Satan, you ingrate!
Coating our hearts with
such beautiful lies!*

Why can't we have Einstein's brain, we complained?
Refusing, not knowing, his own soul was to blame!

*In the darkness, we covered up the truth.
We were lost, dangling away from the root.*

We were trying so hard to resist.
We shook up our hands with ferocious fists!
Of our differences, we made endless lists.
We simply forgot how to exist!
We were so busy, busy, busy.
Our heads couldn't think straight,
we became so dizzy.
So focused on paying for bills and pills,
we forgot one day we would be deadly still.
Don't you know, you will leave it all behind?
Dear God, we were surely out of our minds!
We were so hungry, we needed to feed,
We hurt ourselves in our own aching need.
We numbed it all with processed foods.
In science, we trust, was our
parroted attitude!
We were so focused on how,
we never asked why.
We fed ourselves with such
beautiful lies.

On Light and Sight

"Have they not travelled throughout the land
so their hearts may reason,
and their ears may listen? Indeed, it is not the eyes that are blind,
but it is the hearts in the chests that grow blind." (Quran 22:46)

∞ ∞ ∞

It was in the darkness of
the darkest night,
that,
one day,
we lost
our sight.

Baselessly, we boasted and claimed.
There was no such thing as God's name!
Only because then, we would be so ashamed.
Of what we had done, the things we had maimed!

Breathe. Breathe. Breathe.
Did you forget Who's In Control?
Love, Alone Is the Master of our souls.

Darwin, Einstein, Hawking were all Our slaves.
Tell me, dear one, who were you able to save?

For when the breath came up to the tip of the throat,
all that mattered was what the angels wrote.
They couldn't even leave a final note.
As their souls climbed out,
to Us they would float!

It Is We, Who Take from whomever We Will.
And at once, the human being is dust. Deadly still.
Breathe. Breathe. Breathe.
Did you forget Who's In Control?
Love, Alone Is the Master of our souls.
We were so busy filling things up,
while the heart bled,
a broken cup...

We chased after beauty,
vast mansions on the beach!
For us,
true peace was always
out of reach!
Pardon my abrupt intrusion,
but I think
science proved it all
an optical illusion!
We were so busy
using our brains,
that we forgot to
feel the aching pain!

∞∞∞

Did you forget, dear one,
that your brain lies at the feet...
of our one, indivisible heartbeat?

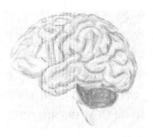

∞∞∞

We threw labels senselessly here and there,
forgetting whose hearts we would truly tear!

Pockets full, we wouldn't empty our cup.
We simply refused to lift each other up!

"Survival of the fittest" became our motto.
As if the descent was like winning the lotto!

We forgot the things that would truly last.
We were stuck, frozen in the past.

We forgot about our deeds, our speech.
Essentially, we forgot how to teach.
And so, the education system crumbled.
We know nothing for sure, our professors mumbled!

Our hands were warm and so were our feet.
Our heads were full, but our hearts barely beat!
"Mommy! Mommy! Do you see what I see?"
"Can't you see I'm working! I'm really busy!"

We became slaves to the rings,
the constant ding-dings.
We forgot how to fly,
forgot we had wings!

We would open our accounts and check the balance.

We nearly lost our hearts, our true talent!

Such harsh words were spoken!
The very homes we lived in became so broken.
We did not uphold our family ties!
All we did was lie, lie, lie.

∞∞∞

In fear,
we barred the windows,
and hid in our homes.
We felt so, so alone.

∞∞∞

We walked by graves so fast.
We did not learn from the tyrants of the past.
We became them ourselves, Lord, we failed in our task!
We did not stop to think their kingdoms did not last.

Did you forget,
you will leave this all behind?
As a human, you are, in fact,
bound by earthly time.

Diseases came,
we thought to make
a name! The cure will
surely be our claim!
To worldly riches and eternal fame!
Even then, we refused to turn back, not
knowing our very humanity was under attack!

So focused on how, we never did ask why.
And life continued to pass us by...

∞∞∞

We became pacifist in our
sheepish quest for truth.
We forgot how to plant a garden,
to de-weed from the root.
Forgetting that we were once a seed,
we dared to ask God
why the world bleeds!

We wanted the world to remember our name.
We didn't look in the mirror first,
we forgot from where we came!
We were so busy touching up
our colorful masks,
we forgot that it's the
soul that lasts!

We condemned to hell in God's name, not
knowing we were already burning
from the pain.

We did not use our voice,
we lied in our speech.
So focused were we on
me, me, me.
We plucked out Your sweet flowers...
forgetting how they only grew in
gentle spring showers.
We clipped the wings of songbirds alike.
Not knowing, not seeing.
They, too, had Divine Light.

We were so scared of being alone.
So we tippy toed through the rooms in our homes.
We drew the curtains in the night real tight.
We forgot how to see, to turn on the light.
Stumbling and mumbling.
"We lost our sight!"
Fumbling and grumbling.
What a fearful fright!

On Light and The Plague

*"Do people think they will be left alone after saying,
'We believe' without being put to the test?"* (Quran 29:2)

∞∞∞

Why don't you put on your mask, they said,
Become like the rest of us, they said, and so,
she put on her mask and became, like
the rest of them, veiled from the world and from
herself. It wasn't until the end of times that
she uncovered how the safety was but an
illusion. For when the masks drop is the
true self revealed...

∞∞∞

Plagues came to remind us,
from where we came.
But we broke the rules,
we stayed the same.
We never thought to
open our eyes.
To question the lies,
to answer the why.
We chose to say goodbye.
Allah Allowed COVID-19...

as a warning for us to
slow down and breathe.
It was a Divine Prescription
for humanity, since we wouldn't
open our eyes and see.
He sent it down as a Mercy.
For us to develop immunity.
To realize how precious is the gift,
to breathe! The hospitals are not
equipped, take heed.
Breathe. Breathe. Breathe.
Strengthen your system!
With good sleep,
drink and eat!
Go, take care of your homes.
You need some time to just be alone.
You thought this world was Paradise.
Go home, clean up and open your eyes.
Don't wait until the end of the week!
Keep going, you will get what you seek!
Go home, feel the cool breeze.
Keep a safe distance from the disease.

Six feet apart or six feet under!
Doesn't it really make you wonder?

Don't wait until the end of the week!
Keep going, you will get what you seek!
Wash your hands and don't ever be mean.
Be careful, it's easy to get unclean!

Make sure you don't breathe in something bad,
it will only make you sad for the health you once had!

Cover yourself when you go to the store.
Keep others safe, don't yell anymore!

Your mask will make breathing so hard,
just relax, just trust your heart!

If you get sick, call The Healer, dear seed.
He Will Surely Help you breathe.
Around the world,
orphans and widows bleed.
Yet, we are the ones in need.

Parts of our body began to die.
Still we thought in our arrogance,
we could survive!
Were we a bunch of sheep?
When will we wake up
from a sleep, so deep?
We used it as an excuse to be so lazy!
Wasting away on Netflix, weren't we crazy!

My love, it's not a coin toss!
Why will you choose such a big loss?

Moms and Dads left out of their
homes, no one to bury them out
of fear of sickness, alone.

It was in our most selfish greed,
that the earth screamed out,
"I can't breathe, I can't breathe!"

Please, dear Lord, they won't let me be!
They refuse to give me what I so desperately need!
No water to drink, no food to eat!
Please, please, please!
Set me free, set me free!

∞∞∞

A flavor of The Last Day,
children's hair will turn
an ashy gray.
There will be nothing left
to say.
A pregnant mother
will drop her
weight...
By then, it will be
far too late.

All that will matter
is who followed the
Right Way.

On Light and Unity

∞∞∞

Are we merely bodies?
Have we lost sight of the whole?
Be honest, put a scalpel to the
soul. Ask yourself, in silence,
what is the worthy goal?

∞∞∞

Oh, I believe in luck, but why,
oh why, do I still feel so stuck!
It must be the universe giving me a sign!
But wait, the universe is also bound by time!

There has to be Someone who made it all.
Someone Who Catches us
when we slip and fall...
Someone Who Has
No beginning,
no end...

Someone Who Could
Be your Forever
Best Friend!
Someone who
Makes trees grow
from tiny little seeds,
Someone Who
Takes Care of all
the worlds' needs!
Why do dead flowers come back to life,
every spring, we pluck out fruits so ripe…
Why do we let out
the deepest sighs?
Why do we hold our hearts to cry?
When we come up with an idea,
Is it a neurotransmitter or two?
That's a very, very big clue!
Is there anything
you can prove?

∞∞∞

Call it science or
call it Signs,
All true knowledge
Is from
The Divine.
The Constant, in a world
of Variables…
Allah, Lord of all
The Worlds!

∞∞∞

Our hands we refuse to raise, not
seeing the nerves in our brains
doing the praise!

In Allah's Hands are all of our
hearts, who are we chasing,
we're so...
far
a
p
a
r
t
.

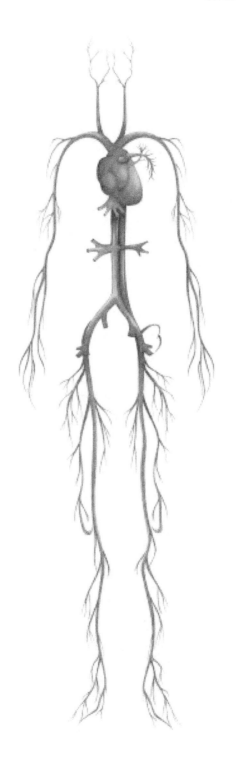

On Light and The Key

*"And those who strive for Us,
We will surely guide them to Our ways.
And indeed, Allah Is With the doers of good."*
(Quran 29:69)

∞∞∞

Won't you ask for the key?
How did you learn to see?
You wake up with so
Much joy! Before the
sun, Like the whole
world's a
toy!
How did you
Drop the
weight, tell
me! Was it an
epiphany?
No, no!
I've been
chipping away for
six years, you see!
To give up bad habits,
to do
good deeds.
To grow a tree...

From a
tiny
little
seed.
Ya Seen.
Wal Quranil
Hakeem.
Here's the secret,
come close!
To how
my heart is
an eternal
red rose.
In my ignition,
I put the key,
Allah
Took Over,
Had Mercy
on me!
He Gifted me
with how to
breathe!
With pure water to
drink and good food
to eat!
I am
free.

∞∞∞

Lord of
Abraham,
Moses,
Jesus and Muhammad.
Peace be upon them all.

The love of these noble messengers will catch us
when we fall. Through the ages, the same message
has come. It is we who turned Love away, refused
to succumb.

After the
hard
labor
and
the
earthly
toil,
it'll be
you and
me beneath
the soil.

On Light and Signs

"We will show them Our signs in the universe and within themselves until it becomes clear to them that this Quran is the truth. Is it not enough that your Lord is a Witness over all things?" (Quran 41:53)

∞∞∞

Quick, go
clean your room!
Is it the brain, the moon or a
baby in its mother's womb? Well, to
me, looks like they're
singing One Tune...

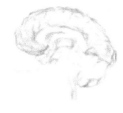  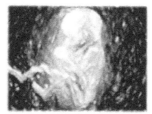

∞∞∞

Quick, go
clean
your
room!
Before
it is
you,
lying
alone
in the
tomb.
Train, train, train!
Oh soul, be quick to
claim your fame!
I promise, I promise!
Nothing is
yet
out
of
r
a
n
g
e.

On Light and The Sun

"Among His signs are the day and the night, the sun and the moon. Do not prostrate to the sun or the moon, but prostrate to Allah, Who created them 'all', if you 'truly' worship Him alone." (Quran 41:37)

When we drop the masks and rise,
when we toss aside all the beautiful lies,
when we no longer have to wear a disguise,
we will soon know the sun has never left our side!

My dear, you are not the sum of your thoughts!
You were never something to be owned or bought!

Let's throw away the blanket of the night!
It is finally time to let it shine bright!
Let's cast away the veil and regain our sight!
What is waiting is Pure, pure Light!

Soon, we will come to see.
It was not the sun who moved!
Wow, can you really believe?

It was me and you.

∞∞∞

For the filter to work, it must be clean
Like the RAC or the brain, I mean!
Or even the barrier
between the seas, so
I think it's time to get
on our knees!
To cry, to beg,
to plead and to
plead!

Greatness is not in shape or size,
Greatness is not stooping down to lie.
Honoring the orphan, and community ties.
Greatness is having the courage to try!

My, oh my, is this goodbye?
Wait, oh wait for the butterfly!

Here's a little thought that might help you see.
The bigger your nose, the more you can breathe!

∞∞∞

Let's be free, free, free!
To drink, to eat, to get what we need!

Let's bring back our childhood curiosities!
That long-lost time when the windows were clean!
Each breath is a burden that we must release.

To truly be free, we must plant a seed!
There's nothing this Divine Breath won't let us attain!
Hurry, oh hurry, let's win this silly game!

On Light and The Multiverse

"We built the universe with great might,
and We are certainly expanding it…"
(Quran 51:47)

∞∞∞

That physicist, Max Heisenberger,
was just another one of Allah's workers.
Through observation, he found,
the only real things were vibrations,
were sound! The proton and him were one.
It's all United, there's nowhere to run!

∞∞∞

The entire universe was once a single seed.
Before it was smoke, water and heat!
Before it burst itself in two!
Like a cell dividing
to make me and you! The flowers, the birds,
the bees and the trees. The tiny fleas,
the roaring seas. Even the Milky Way Galaxy!
Until the Divine breath said to it,
Be.
Pure Love Created it for you and for me.

We remembered You, and so we could see!
We have the whole universe in our little pinky!
Everything has Love's signature, dear seed!
Prophet Atom, the first human seed,
the heart, the womb
that made you and
me!

It's all part of a Divine pattern!
The earth's orbit, the rings of Saturn!
The solar system is like our eyes!
The pupil's the sun, my, oh my!

We use the fancy word flow,
For when we come to know,
We're more than just bodies,
We let our souls show!

∞∞∞

There are miracles everywhere!
In ourselves, up at the
skies we stare! It's all a giant
ball. Love will catch us when
we slip and
fall!
Up, down, up down,
it's a circus all around!
Our universe is like an
amusement park, a
game, to be fair!
Of how much He Loves,
how much He Cares!
It's okay, there's nothing to fear!

Hands up, like our brain's hemispheres!
Our ribcage looks like a pair of wings,
as we sit on our knees. Hands up, we
surrender, submit, to be free!
Every atom spells His Divine...
Name. Is it an M or a W, we are all
the same! Our body point down
to the earth, you see! But our hearts
point to the heavens,
up, to be free!

On Light and The Cure

"And when I am ill, it is [Allah] who cures me."
(Quran 26:80)

∞∞∞

Dear Lord, Give us water,
and good food to eat!
Or we will forever remain
helpless, tiny little
seeds!

Breathe. Breathe. Breathe.
Did you forget Who's In Control?
Love, Alone, Is the Master
of our souls.
At last, at last, I can finally see!
What perfect unity!

Wow, oh wow, so many colors,
shapes and sizes! Hear me, I say!
What beautiful disguises!
That bird that just flew us by,
it was a sign, my oh my!
What a brilliant,
clever disguise!
I'm so glad
I opened up
my eyes!

I'll put good things
in my belly!
I don't want my brain
to be smelly!

Like a superhero,
I'll put on my cape!
I'll drink lots
of water for
Allah's Sake!

The fruits are like
our body
shapes!
The oranges and
even the grapes!

And yummy
vegetables too!
Avocadoes
and carrots are so
good for you!

The really expensive
beauty creams
are all just elaborate
money-making schemes!
For every disease
there is a
natural cure.
Of this, I am very,
very sure.

The One
Who Makes
the butterflies soar!

The One
Who Takes Care
of the earth's core!

The Only One
my heart beats for,
never Left me alone,
He Gave me the tour!

It's the fox that
tries to lure,
with fake
promises,
to be sure!

That
much
pain,
I can't
endure...

Like a lion, at it I will roar!
You don't control me
anymore!

I will raise my
hands and soar!
I will knock on
every single door!

∞∞∞

Breathe in the good,

leave the bad out!

I will be aware,

I will move about!

On Light and The Mercy

And We have not sent you, [O Muhammad],
except as a mercy to the worlds. (Quran 21:107)

∞∞∞

Did you stop
for a moment
to think?
How Allah Helped
the desert Bedouins!
In it's a lesson,
a definite link.
If you would just slow down
and stop
to think!

∞∞∞

In darkness, they would sing and dance!
Burying baby girls without a chance!
Alcohol would be their chosen drink!
They never even stopped to think!

So Love Sent
down a special hope,
remind them to hold on
to Its Loving Rope.

He Himself Chose
The Last Prophet ﷺ
our beloved Rasul,
Light spread,
from Makkah to
the rest of the world!
An orphan, he ﷺ was born,
As a child, his ﷺ heart was torn,
He ﷺ lost his mom at six, it's true!
his grandfather soon after, too…
In the Hira cave, where
he ﷺ would go meditate,
Allah's Angel Jibril came, life
would never, ever be the same.
In the name of your Lord, recite!
Don't be afraid, open up to the Light!
It was an uphill climb,
it took a whole 23 years' time!
Those who submit themselves,
Who turn to God Alone for help.
With fairness, they always dealt!
Early Muslims, how full they felt!
When Allah's Command Came,
they did not stay the same.
They would obey, follow
The Right Way
no matter what
others would
do or
say.
The body
was tortured
and slain,
So much blood,
so much pain…
Yet, their souls they chose to save!

They were heroes, they were brave.
In their hearts, they knew: the promise
of their beloved Lord was true.

His ﷺ wife and uncle would soon leave,
he ﷺ had so much loss to grieve, yet
he ﷺ was the master of chivalry, to
the worlds, the most beautiful mercy ﷺ.
Allah's Prophet ﷺ fell
to his knees, on
his companion,
he ﷺ asked
to lean,
as he ﷺ made his way, to the
orchard, where his baby boy lay, his
blessed heart ﷺ breaking from the pain,
His ﷺ tears pouring down, like rain,
As his ﷺ beloved child passed away, as
he ﷺ gently laid him down in his little grave.
His ﷺ son never woke up from his sleep...
His ﷺ heart was sad, and his ﷺ eyes did weep,
but he ﷺ only said what would please his Lord,
he ﷺ has the ultimate reward!

∞∞∞

Allah, Our Lord Himself Swore,
His beloved's ﷺ character, was the Door,
for you to never, ever be alone anymore.
He ﷺ tied stones around his belly, you see,
The Beloved of God ﷺ would be so hungry.
He ﷺ would often be found fasting, the
Prince ﷺ of this world and the everlasting.
His companions would weep, their leader, ﷺ
on a rough straw mat would gently sleep...

I am a traveler, he would say...
This world, for me, has no weight.
I will rest beneath the shadow of this
tree, on my way home...
To be
free.

The greatest teacher that ever lived,
He would always forgive, give, give.
He taught us that you will never
believe, until you love for
one another what
for yourself,
you keep.
Kindness beautifies a thing,
kind of like a diamond ring!

A house in the
middle of Paradise,
for the one who
gives up
lies.

∞∞∞

The most beautiful man to ever be,
Love's most beautiful seed,
the savior of all, not just
humanity...

∞∞∞

I will cut my heart
ya habib, for you, in two!
I hope we can meet really soon,
to share some Jannah macaroons!

Allah Said if you love Me, follow
Rahmatul Lil 'Aaalameen!
Lord of
Abraham,
Moses,
Jesus and Muhammad.
Peace be upon them all.
The love of these noble messengers will not
let us fall. Through the ages, the same message
has come. It is we who turned Love down,
refused to succumb.

On Light and Effort

"That man will only have what he has worked towards,
and that his effort shall soon be seen, and that
in the end, he will be repaid full for it, and that
to your Lord alone Is the ultimate
return of all things."
(Quran 53:39-42)

∞∞∞

He won't ask for your resume,
Not even your grades! If
you do one good deed,
it'll multiply,
dear seed.
Plants will slowly grow,
with hundreds of seeds to show!
Such Generosity.
From the One,
Above all need.

∞∞∞

Force times work is power,
Allah's Help comes with
effort, little flower!

If we came down to
survive,
Is creativity just
a lie?
Rumi, Shakespeare, Monet,
Their soul's works
Are here,
to stay!
Let's not forget
Audrey Hepburn,
So little time, so
much to learn!
Her light was
inner beauty,
Humanitarian work was
her duty.

∞∞∞

Einstein saw a dream,
That told him what
Time Really Means!
They called
It
His
Miracle
Year,
For my servant,
Indeed, I Am near.

Like farmers, we will harvest
our seeds, And Allah Will
Multiply all our good deeds!

On Light and Power

*"…and We strengthened their hearts when they
stood up and declared, 'Our Lord is the
Lord of the heavens and the earth. We will
never call upon any god besides Him,
or we would truly be uttering
an outrageous lie.'"*
(Quran 18:14)

∞ ∞ ∞

I will be strong,
like Hadhrat Umar Farooq,
Who conquered the world
with very little troops! The
Prophet's companions
came in Peace…
To take away
Jerusalem's keys.

Hadhrat Umar Farooq,
let his servant ride
at the front of the group.
He entered the city
on foot himself.
Who was the king, and
who was the help?

This is real,
it's not a story!
To Allah Alone,
Belongs all the Glory!
With Allah on his side,
the greatest empires
had to say goodbye!
Really, wow!
Really, how!
Oh how!
Asked the
kings and queens
of Persia and Rome,
As desert Arabs took
their palaces, their homes!

On Light and Nobility

"O humanity! Indeed, We created you
from a male and a female, and
made you into peoples and tribes so
that you may ⌐get to¬ know one another. Surely
the most noble of you in the sight of Allah is
the most righteous among you.
Allah is truly All-Knowing, All-Aware."
(Quran 49:13)

At
times
I wish
to be
a little
black
seed.
In the
hands of
Hadhrat Bilal the
first muezzin to lead!
He drank water, had
the best food to eat!
His footsteps were
heard in Paradise,
ahead of the
Prophet's ﷺ
himself,
bona fide!

∞∞∞

Allah Told us When He Said Be.
We Made you into nations and tribes.
So you could see.
See, and be free,
so you could
see Me.

∞∞∞

For Me,
The Most Beautiful Seed
Is One Devoted to me,
Unseen.

And I have Not
Created Jinn or
Mankind except to
Worship Me Alone,

Said Allah,
The Lord of
The Mighty
Throne.

On Light and Epiphany

"…so the magicians fell down in prostration.
They said, "We have believed in the Lord of
Aaron and Moses." [Pharaoh] said, "You believed him
before I gave you permission. Indeed, he is your leader who has
taught you magic.
So I will surely cut off
your hands and your feet on opposite sides, and I will
crucify you on the trunks of palm trees, and you will
surely know which of us is more severe in [giving]
punishment and more enduring…" They said
"Never will we prefer you over what has
come to us of clear proofs and [over]
He who created us.
So decree whatever you are to decree. You
can only decree for this worldly life. Indeed, we
have believed in our Lord that He May Forgive
us our sins and what you compelled us [to do] of
magic. And Allah is better and more enduring.""
(Quran 20:70-73)

∞ ∞ ∞

The measured rain, the window stains!
The huge airplanes, the Choo-Choo train!
The one-way lane, the pain and the fame,
it's all the same! It's one big game!

∞∞∞

So here we are, dear Lord, bowed
in humility, gratitude and shame.
Here we are.
How desperately we have longed
to hear Your Blessed Name!

These tears are like
water for the soul.
Pleasing You is our
One and only goal.

Our shoulders are
too weak to carry
burdens on our own.
Strength and Power,
we found, Is Always
In You, Alone.
The Owner of the
Mighty Throne.
And yet, You Have
Never Left us to be
on our own.
You Give.
The Divine breath is
why we all live.
You Take from
whomever You Will.
At once, the human
being is dust,
deadly still.
Our Provider, Our Sustainer!
Your Love Is all we need!

You Alone are
The Praiseworthy,
Above all need.
Your Love Is The
Love that feeds!
The flowers, the birds,
the bees and the trees.
Oh, what did I just read!
My friend, remember to breathe!
The tiny fleas, the roaring seas!
Even the Milky Way
Galaxy!
Creation is
in pairs, you see...
even you and even me!
Don't be sad,
He's Not far away!
He Hears and Sees way
more than you say!
No, my love, don't be afraid!
He's Closer to you than
your jugular vein! Now
that all is said and done,
there is nowhere left to run!

∞∞∞

You Will Roll up the
heavens in Your Right Hand.
Beyond spacetime, Yours
Alone Is The Command.

The ingrate will bite his hands
and wish to be dust!

The Court Will be silent in front of
The Most Merciful, The Most Just.
Allahu Akbar.
No matter who we are,
Allah Is Greater.
Love Is Our One,
Our Only Creator.

∞∞∞

Our hearts You Have Cleaned,
by Your Infinite Mercy!
We are finally free! We can see!
Under One, the banner of unity.

At last, at last, we let ourselves breathe!
It was only then that we heard
the heartbeat...

∞∞∞

Allah, we thank you for our sight!
This world is truly light upon light!
Our Master, Our Maker,
we have nothing to give!
So we give up our hearts,
the reason we live.
We pledge to become a clear
mirror for Your Creation.
We know it is only then we will
heal, as one, united nation.
It was all an
elaborate lie!

∞∞∞

Like the sun,
once again,
from the darkness
we will rise!
We will tuck the
phones away,
we will never,
ever be afraid!
We will use
our hearts to feed.
We will make time
to drink and to eat!
All of us, together now,
One
comm-
unity!
We will uproot
the silly lies,
the greed.
We, too, will lovingly
plant the seed.
Our children will thank us
for giving our home
what it needs.

∞∞∞

Oh Allah, all praise and thanks
is for You, Alone.
For You Are The Lord
of The Mighty Throne.

Oh soul, take heed.
At last, at last!
We can
finally,
see!
There is no me
and you, only us.
United we stand,
in God we trust!

∞∞∞

My dear, doesn't it feel so good to breathe?
To give yourself water to drink and food to eat?
You might feel a sudden jolt.
Kind of like a
powerful electric volt. Fear not, like the
springtime bloom, your heart, too,
will soon sing the same Tune.

With your own hands, can you create a flea?
What about an itty-bitty barley seed?
Did you stop for a moment to think?
About the food you eat, the water you drink?
All the worlds have been tamed for you!
Just imagine the sun came and sat in your room!

Don't you remember, you were once a seed?
How could you forget My Love, forget to see?
I Created you, Invented you and Fashioned you.
This, I Swear, is the Ultimate Truth.

Breathe. Breathe. Breathe.
In every breath, you are so
in need.

Oxygen comes in,
CO2's on the loose!
It benefits the environment, too,
not just me and you!
It's all connected, silly goose!
Like a scavenger hunt, to give you clues.
0+1 is One.
Wow, that's a relief, thanks a ton!
Now that all is said and done,
there is nowhere left to run!

On Light and Time

By time, indeed mankind is in loss,
Except for those who have believed and done righteous deeds,
and advised each other to truth and advised each other to patience.

(Quran 103:1-3)

∞∞∞

The One Who Made Time, Makes time for you.

∞∞∞

He's Been Here all along!
He Promises to Forgive you,
no matter what you do wrong!
It's true, it's true!
You're alive, that's a clue!
Of how much hope He Has in you!
It's true, it's true!
His Promise is to Make you brand new!
With lots of light energy,
electrons transform inside you and me!
They're protons now, a quantum leap!
They were spinning in a circle,
with negative charge, but for my Allah,
nothing is hard. *Be still, my beating heart!*

The faster you clean,
the more you erase!
The quicker you'll get
the most beautiful taste, of
what's waiting for you,
when you win the race!
You are so loved, my dear.
Indeed, for all My servants,
I Am Near.

Your own cells
are in His Control.
Hurry, oh hurry,
To save your own
soul!

How can I make time to see?
Well, did you hear of relativity?
Now that you so kindly asked,
I'll explain it really fast!

My dear, what you see in the sky, is
more than a 100 billion light years wide!
And that is just the lowest heaven!
A total of which there
are Seven!
Each is a tiny ring
Compared to the one before...
In the Sahara Desert, to be sure!
String Theory helped us explore,
there are other dimensions in store.
These are signs we cannot ignore.
Nothing can scare us anymore!
Above, the Noble Kursiy and The Throne,
Allah, Who's Never, ever left us alone.
The angels ascend in a single day,
Like a thousand years for us!

Don't be afraid! Under the veil of
Pure Light, you will
time travel,
day or night!
Have Hope and
have fear,
indeed, to you, *He Is Near*.
He Will Always Answer your call,
so be brave and stand up tall!
All of existence is His to own, and
you don't even need a telephone!
He responds to those in despair,
and even those who need...
a simple shoe repair!

A staff is not a staff,
and fire can be
so cool, it'll
make you laugh!
Allah Made
the Rules,
everything
submits to
Him, isn't
that cool?
True religion came
to relieve your burden,
you see. Beyond the
darkness of the curtain,
there would be Me.

On Light and Rituals

*"Recite what has been revealed to you of the Scripture;
keep up the prayer: prayer restrains outrageous
and unacceptable behavior. Remembering Allah
is greater: Allah knows everything
you are doing.*

*Argue only in
the best way with the
People of the Book, except with those
of them who act unjustly. Say, 'We believe in what was
revealed to us and in what was revealed to you; our God and
your God are one [and the same]; we are devoted to Him.' "*
(Quran 29:45-46)

∞∞∞

We must take care of our brainstem,
if we want our immune system to be
able to defend! The Shahada is like
breathing and Salah is just like eating!

Zakat purifies your wealth, so you can
take good care of your home, your health!
Fasting is a shield like the Earth's
magnetosphere, it protects us from
our desires, hear, hear! Like our
white blood cells...

Our body calls on them for special help!
We return to The Kaaba at Hajj, standing
before Allah, The Final Judge. The Quran
was sent down as rain, to wash away all the
aching pain! Allah's Plan Is So Perfect, just
relax, it'll all be worth it! May we never be alone,
may Allah Take us all the way home.
Ameen!

∞∞∞

Oh, all the rituals really make
sense! Soul, mind and body,
we must completely cleanse.

Do it for His Sake, and genius awaits.
It's in your DNA, your superhuman fate.
Let's take our longing for perfection and beauty,
make heaven in our homes for the angels to see.

Throw the junk away, it's nearly too late.
Let's get back to our genetic weight!

Go out, look around and discover!
Beautiful things only you can uncover!
Breathing will be your ultimate tool.
Not just for the things you learn in school,
to the secrets of the universe, isn't that cool!

With the Quran in hand, against
injustice, you'll take a firm stand!
There will be freedom in all the lands,
From The North Pole to the desert sands!

When the batteries are charged,
it will be time to leave.

We know it's soon, that
we will be free.
From the cocoon,
we have struggled to flee.
We can't wait to get out so
we can finally see!
Love,
The
Ultimate
Reality!

On Light and The Grave

"When the soul of a dying man comes up to
his throat, and you are at that time looking on,
And Our angels are nearer to him than you,
but you do not see. Now, if you are not
subject to Our Will 'as you claim',
bring that soul back,
if what you say is
true..."
(Quran 56:83-87)

*You will certainly pass
from stage to stage..."*
(Quran 84:19)

It's time to turn the page...

*Will our graves be like
a bed, nice and snug,
will it give us a...
welcoming hug?
Will the Quran come
to our defense?*

In the form of a
bright best friend?

When it comes time to cash
out, who will hear your
screams and shouts?
For the real life ahead
what did you send?
What will be your true end?

May Allah Protect us!
United we stand, in
God, we trust!

On Light and Separation

*"Were My revelations not recited to you,
but you used to deny them?" They will cry,
"Our Lord! Our ill-fate took hold of us, so
we became a misguided people. Our Lord!*

*Take us out of this ˻Fire˼. Then if we ever return
˻to denial˼, we will truly be wrongdoers." He
Will Say, "Be despised in there and do
not speak to Me." (Quran 23:105-108)*

All the worlds will surely fade.
We beg You, Allah,
The Eternal Refuge,
Grant us your shade!

Will we be so locked in our rage,
that when the time comes,
we will fall from the stage?
Will we be able to fly?
Our All-Knowing Creator
will ask us why! We burned
off our wings without a sigh.
We closed our eyes.

We said goodbye.
We chose the
beautiful
lie.

What a terrifying sight, I say!
How we ducked our heads and ran
far away. From a Lord Who Wrote
Upon The Throne, what prevails
over My Wrath Is
My Mercy
alone.

On Light and Reunion

"…'[But] you, soul at peace, Return to your Lord,
well pleased with Him and well pleasing to
Him. So join My servants, and
enter My Paradise.'"
(Quran 89:27-30)

I, for one, hope to choose the right way.
When it's Allah's Will, I'll fly from the stage.
To this mortal mask, I'll say goodbye. And
Everlasting Beauty will welcome its new butterfly.

"We can dwell in Paradise, wherever we will!
The perfect reward for those who do well!
The angels will be at the Gates to see,
us being crowned as kings and queens!

We will never be bored again,
we can meet all of our true friends!
Rivers of milk, wine and honey,
No, there will be no need for money!

Castles with infinite rooms…

We will see Allah
like we see the full moon!

Faces will be shining bright!
Full of our Lord's Eternal Light!
What a breathtakingly beautiful sight!
Finally. Light upon light.

"Peace be upon you, for what
you patiently endured!"
You will have your
fullest reward!

All Praise and thanks to
The Lord of The Mighty Throne.
"Excellent indeed is the final home."
(Quran 13:24)

On Light and Submission

"'This day have those who cover up the truth have given up all hope of undermining your faith. So do not fear them; fear Me! Today I have perfected your faith for you, completed My Favor upon you and chosen Islam as your way...'"
(Quran 5:3)

We see what
life truly means.
Peace. Peace. Peace.
We have submitted, willingly!
Shape us, dear God, into who we were
meant to be! Alhamdulillahi Rabbil 'Aalameen!

∞∞∞

"As for those who repent, believe, and do good deeds, they are the ones whose evil deeds Allah will change into good deeds. For Allah is All-Forgiving, Eternally Compassionate." (Quran 25:70)

∞∞∞

All praise and thanks is for Allah, the Lord of all the worlds.

Light Upon Light!

اللَّهُ نُورُ السَّمَاوَاتِ وَالْأَرْضِ مَثَلُ نُورِهِ كَمِشْكَاةٍ فِيهَا مِصْبَاحٌ الْمِصْبَاحُ فِي زُجَاجَةٍ الزُّجَاجَةُ كَأَنَّهَا كَوْكَبٌ دُرِّيٌّ يُوقَدُ مِن شَجَرَةٍ مُبَارَكَةٍ زَيْتُونِةٍ لَّا شَرْقِيَّةٍ وَلَا غَرْبِيَّةٍ يَكَادُ زَيْتُهَا يُضِيءُ وَلَوْ لَمْ تَمْسَسْهُ نَارٌ نُّورٌ عَلَى نُورٍ يَهْدِي اللَّهُ لِنُورِهِ مَن يَشَاءُ وَيَضْرِبُ اللَّهُ الْأَمْثَالَ لِلنَّاسِ وَاللَّهُ بِكُلِّ شَيْءٍ عَلِيمٌ

Allah Is the Light of the heavens and the earth. His Light is like this: there is a niche, and in it a lamp, the lamp inside a glass, a glass like a glittering star, fueled from a blessed olive tree from neither east nor west, whose oil almost gives light even when no fire touches it – light upon light – Allah Guides whoever He wills all the way to his Light; Allah Draws such comparisons for people Allah Has full knowledge of everything. (Quran 24:35)

∞∞∞

One Final Note.

If this book is one you read,
While I still breathe,
Please pray for this little seed,
It's Allah's Test, to see,
Will I practice what I preach,
Help me be free, free, free!
If you hear news of my last breath,
For the only thing certain is death,
Pray for green birds that are never alone,
Flying around The Most Merciful's Throne,
No more pain, just peace above, as I
reunite with my eternal Love.
Rasulullah's ﷺ hand, to me,
so close, forever home in
Al-Firdaws.
Ameen!

∞ ∞ ∞

When you are complimented,
say all good is from Allah.
The Most Merciful and The Most Loving.
He Is As-Shakoor, the Most Appreciative, of our little efforts.
Allah Gave me a mouth to appreciate Him, hands to raise
to Him and senses to see the worlds around me. There is
nothing I can do that will ever equate to His Infinite blessings
upon me. It is not because of who I am, it is because of who
He Is. How can you not love Him? The Most Beautiful, the
Most Perfect, the One Who Is Above all need, yet He Boasts
about us to His Angels, when we use the blessings He Gave us
to Praise Him! Allahu Akbar! Allah Is Love. Ashhadu an Laa
ilaaha il Allah wa ashhadu anna Muhammadur Rasulullah!
My Eternal Love. The heart has come home. It is full.

∞∞∞

To bring your heart back to life,
you must shock it with paddles,
you see. And when you forget,
just breathe.

∞∞∞

The Prophet's ﷺ *Prayer*

Allahumma j'al-fi-qalbi-nuran- wa-fi-basri-nuran- wa-fi-sam'i-
nuran- wa-an-yamini-nuran- wa-an-yasaari-nuran- wa-fawqi-
nuran- wa-tahti-nuran- wa-amaami-nuran- wa-khalfi-nuran- wa-
j'al-li-nuran- wa-fi-lisaani-nuran- wa-'asabi-nuran- wa-lahmi-
nuran- wa-dami-nuran- wa-sha'ri-nuran- wa-bashari-nuran- wa-
j'al-fi-nafsi-nuran- wa-a'zim-li-nuran- allahumma- 'atini-nuran.
O Allah!
Grow light/knowing in my heart, light in my eyes,
light in my ears,
light on my right,
light on my left,
light above me,
light beneath me,
light before me,
light behind me;
and grow for me light/knowing-- light in my tongue,
light in my sinews (muscle)
light in my flesh (soft tissue),
light in my blood,
light in my hair,
light in my form and appearance,
light in my nafs—sense of self,
make this light flexible and strong.
O Allah gift me with the light already present inside and out.

A Note of Gratitude

For you Rasulullah, Blessings be upon you, your family and companions. Habibullah, The Beloved of God. It is your nur, ya Rasulullah, that is continuously lighting the straight path for us. Let my parents be sacrificed for you, for your smile, oh Rasulullah! Because of you, I got to know the Prophets Abraham, Moses and Jesus, peace be upon them all. Alhamdulillah for Mama, my love, my everything. Alhamdulillah for Papa. My two super-heroes. With continuous effort and prayer, your dreams have made me realize that Allah Sees potential in us even when we don't see it ourselves. A reminder of Allah's Infinite Mercy. My dear Dada-Abbu, may Allah Pardon you and Grant you Al-Firdaws! Let's meet there again, in sha Allah! All my life I wanted one older sister, and Allah Blessed me with so many. Alhamdulillah for these gems, Amna and Zeinab, Sara, Nada, Maham, Biha, Sila, Subhan, Nafisa, Sakeena, Muhammad, Ahmad, Yusuf, Safa, Hasana, Yunus, Aaila, Leena, Reetaj, Talia, Yacob, Adam, Mahrukh, Amna, Awaab, Huda, Yashfa, Mutashma, Hamza and Rani. Thank You for teaching me how to love. To Dr. Brind, who gave me priceless treasures. Alhamdulillah for every human, every child, every chirping bird, every blade of grass and every butterfly that brought me back to My Beloved. It is your forgiving shoulders that I stand on, today. By His Mercy. Alhamdulillah.

Made in the USA
Las Vegas, NV
17 November 2023

81048171R00059